Banjo

for beginners

Contents

An Easy Beginning Method

Copyright © MMI Alfred Publishing Co., Inc.
All rights reserved. Printed in USA.
ISBN 0-7390-1103-0 (Book)
ISBN 0-7390-1104-9 (Book & CD)
ISBN 0-7390-1105-7 (CD)

This book was acquired, edited and produced
by Workshop Arts, Inc., the publishing arm of
the National Guitar Workshop.
Nathaniel Gunod, editor and acquisition editor
Michael Rodman, editor
Gary Tomassetti, music typesetter and assistant editor
Timothy Phelps, interior design and photography
CD recorded at Bar None Studios, Northford, CT

Cover instrument photo courtesy of Gibson.

TONY TRISCHKA

About the Author

Tony Trischka has helped to redefine the banjo, its technical vocabulary and the contexts in which it is heard. To date he has recorded 12 solo albums featuring artists such as David Grisman, Pete Seeger, Béla Fleck, Jerry Douglas, William S. Burroughs, Charles Osgood, Alison Krauss, the Violent Femmes and members of R.E.M. Tony's musical travels have taken him from Broadway to Croatia to New Zealand, and he has performed with bluegrass bands, avant-garde jazz groups, symphony orchestras and percussion ensembles. He has appeared on the radio shows *A Prairie Home Companion, Mountain Stage, Fresh Air* and *Weekend Edition*, performed with John Denver on the CBS *Hallmark Hall of Fame* production *Foxfire*, starring Hume Cronyn and Jessica Tandy, and was profiled, along with Béla Fleck, on *CBS News Sunday Morning*. Tony is also in demand as a teacher, and he has numerous instructional books and videos to his credit. He has been a columnist for a number of acoustic music publications and has written liner notes for Béla Fleck, Alison Krauss and many others.

PHOTO • TIMOTHY PHELPS

Track 1

A compact disc is available for this book. This disc can make learning with this book easier and more enjoyable. This symbol will appear next to every example that is on the CD. Use the CD to help insure that you are capturing the feel of the examples, interpreting the rhythms correctly, and so on. The track numbers below the symbols correspond directly to the example you want to hear. Track 1 will help you tune your banjo. Have fun!

Introduction

Welcome to what may well be the first banjo book you've ever owned. If you're reading this, you're curious about five-string bluegrass banjo—maybe even smitten. You might have heard the funky lightning of Earl Scruggs's 1950 Mercury recording of *Foggy Mountain Breakdown*. Perhaps you saw Béla Fleck and the Flecktones burn down the stage in a jazz-rock-bluegrass meltdown. Maybe your uncle's in a bluegrass band and you wondered how anyone could play that fast. No matter how you made it, I'm happy you're here.

I got "banjo bit" really bad in 1962 and haven't recovered since. I was thirteen, owned a copy of Pete Seeger's seminal banjo instruction book and was at that point working things out on my guitar (which, in desperation, I had tuned like a banjo). That Christmas, my parents presented me with a Christy long-necked banjo. To me, it was an icon—perfectly round with glistening metal brackets and impossibly long strings.

In those days there wasn't much in the way of instructional material for the banjo, just Seeger's book and another by Sonny Osborne of the Osborne Brothers. I was fortunate, though, to have a teacher who bestowed upon me instant enlightenment. Today, there are scads of banjo-related books, magazines, videos and websites, most of which will give you a good introduction to the instrument. With all the five-stringed bounty out there, I'm glad you chose this book to start your journey.

Being a beginner on the banjo is a good thing, because the learning curve is so nearly vertical. This book will take you from ground zero to the outskirts of intermediate bluegrass banjo. Along the way, you may plateau for a bit before making the next leap forward. Don't despair; I've seen it a thousand times, both in myself and in others. You'll feel like you'll never progress any further, and suddenly you find yourself at the next level. Remember to be patient.

This book assumes you know nothing about the banjo. If you can already play a stringed instrument, though, you'll have an advantage in terms of left- and right-hand coordination. You'll begin by learning to strum a few chords, and then you'll use them with right-hand finger patterns. In time, you'll learn how to incorporate melodies into these finger patterns. Later, you'll enhance melodies with left-hand spiffer-uppers like slides, hammer-ons and pull-offs, which will give you a true bluegrass sound. There is a section on practicing, a bit about playing in the key of C and a final section on reading music notation. It doesn't matter how old you are—it's never too late to start. I've taught both ten-year-olds and senior citizens. If at first things seem sloppy, a year later they'll sound better. In fact, it's not a bad idea to record yourself when you first start, and frequently thereafter. Listen to the recordings to gauge the progress you've made. Perhaps most importantly, jam—get together with others and play. Even if you can only strum a few chords and try to remain unobtrusive at jam sessions, get in there and pick. This will quickly accelerate your progress, allow you to incorporate the ideas you learn from this book and magnify your joy in making music.

DEDICATION
This book is dedicated to the memory and music of John Hartford.

ACKNOWLEDGEMENTS
Thanks to Assunta, Sean and Zoe for everything; Lincoln Child, a rascally bounder and banjo-, pizza- and all-around bud, for major editing; Harold Mermelstein and Jack Funt for idea-bouncing, feedback and good natures; Hal Glatzer, my banjo teacher, for showing me the way; Don Weiss, for singing and playing on the CD; and the members of my 2001 Banjo Camp North practicing class for their input on playing along with recordings.

Chapter 1

Listen

First of all, listen, listen, listen! If you already have some favorite banjo players, get their sounds in your ears. In other words, absorb as much as you can. Just let the music wash over you. When I was starting out, I would sit for hours by the family turntable listening to Flatt and Scruggs's classic *Foggy Mountain Banjo*, staring at the artist's depiction of Earl Scruggs's talon-like fingerpicks and letting the warm yellow of the cover add to the electrifying musical ambience coming from the grooves. Unfortunately, times are different now. If you're as busy as I am, you'll probably do most of your listening in your car. Get your dose of listening wherever you can. (See page 47 for some CD sources.)

Listening will enable you to make connections. For instance, after you learn *Cripple Creek* (page 39), you'll find yourself playing a particular lick on the 3rd string. Once you've listened to other tunes, you'll hear this lick popping up all over the place; at the beginning of Earl Scruggs's recording of *Shucking the Corn,* for example, it occurs three times. You will begin to realize that bluegrass tunes are built of phrases that occur in many different songs. The mystery begins to fall away.

Parts of the Banjo

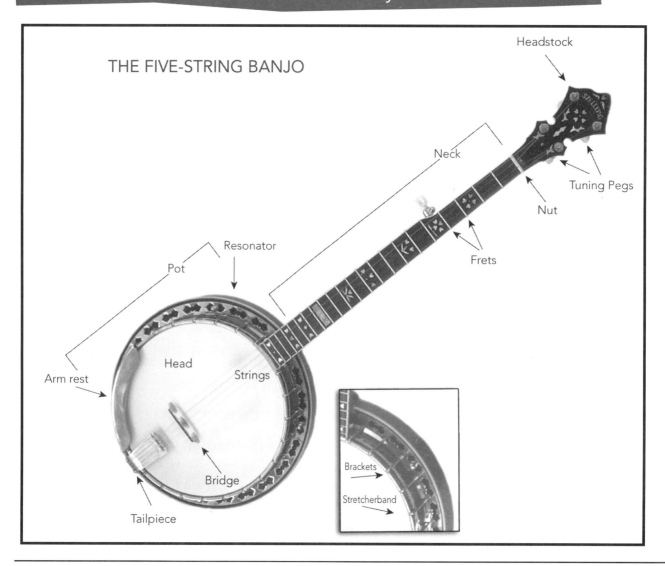

THE FIVE-STRING BANJO

Headstock

Neck

Tuning Pegs

Nut

Frets

Resonator

Pot

Head

Strings

Arm rest

Bridge

Tailpiece

Brackets

Stretcherband

Holding the Banjo

Hold the banjo in a way you find comfortable. When sitting, I usually cradle it in my lap (even though the old song refers to coming from Alabama "with a banjo on my knee"). The neck of the banjo should be slightly inclined from a horizontal position, while the *pot* (drum section of the instrument) should be on its side in a nearly vertical position. Feel free to make subtle adjustments according to what feels best.

If you have a resonator-style banjo, the smooth wood will feel comfortable in your lap. If you have an open-back instrument, you may find that the brackets dig into you a little bit. If this is a problem, fold up a towel, place it in your lap, and set the banjo on top.

Playing while standing requires the use of a strap. This automatically changes the angle of the fingerboard, which may seem awkward at first. At this point, you don't need to worry too much about playing while standing; however, this is the most common position when playing with others, so you should plan on getting used to it.

Sitting with the banjo.

Standing with the banjo.

Tuning Your Banjo

Properly tuning a banjo isn't always easy, but nowadays it's easier than ever before. In the old days, players had to tune their instruments by ear; today, you can save a lot of trouble and achieve excellent results by using an electronic tuner, a relatively inexpensive device that can be purchased at most music stores. Some tuners are more sensitive to the sound of the banjo than others. If you can, try out a tuner before you buy it, and be sure to ask the salesperson to explain and demonstrate its features.

The first thing to know when tuning your instrument is that *pitch*—a note's specific "highness" or "lowness"—is expressed with the first seven letters of the alphabet: A, B, C, D, E, F, G. If you have a don't have an electonic tuner, you can use the old-fashioned method to tune your banjo. The following describes standard bluegrass tuning.

Track 1

Step 1. Using an electronic tuner or other instrument, tune the open (unfingered) 4th string to D by turning the tuning peg as necessary to raise or lower the pitch.

Step 2. *Fret* (press down your finger on) the 4th string at the 5th fret to sound G, and compare this pitch with that of the open 3rd string. Tune the 3rd string until it is in *unison* with (at the same pitch as) the fretted 4th string.

Step 3. Fret the 3rd string at the 4th fret to sound B and compare it to the open 2nd string. Tune the 2nd string until it is in unison with the fretted 3rd string.

Step 4. Fret the 2nd string at the 3rd fret to sound D and compare it with the open 1st string. Tune the 1st string until it is in unison with the fretted 2nd string.

Step 5. Fret the 5th fret of the 1st string to sound G and compare it with the open 5th string.

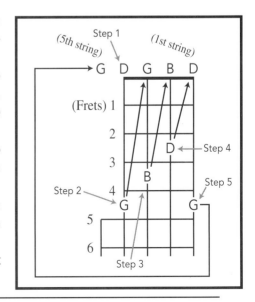

Banjo music is most often notated in a system called *tablature* (or "TAB"). Tablature is handy because, unlike standard music notation, it relates specifically to the instrument for which it's written. In banjo TAB, each line of a five-line *staff* represents one of the banjo's strings. The bottom line represents the 5th (short) string, the next line up represents the 4th string, the line up from that the 3rd string, and so on.

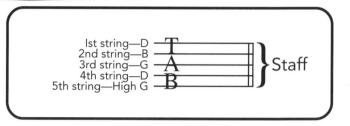

A "0" on the first (top) line, for example, indicates that you should play the 1st string open (not fretted). A "2" on the 3rd line indicates that you should place one of your left-hand fingers on the 3rd string at the 2nd fret.

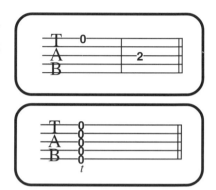

Right-hand indications are found beneath the staff. A "*t*" means to play with the thumb, an "*i*" with the index finger and an "*m*" with the middle finger. The example at right directs the player to *strum* (play with a quick sweeping motion) all the open strings with the thumb.

Measures and Beats
Music is divided into *measures* or *bars,* marked off by vertical lines called *bar lines* (see Example 1 below). In most tunes, measures represent equal units of musical time. Measures, in turn, are divided into equal units of time called *beats*. Think of the beats in a measure in terms of your own heartbeat—a steady, even, recurring pulse.

Quarter Notes and Eighth Notes
In most bluegrass music, the value (that is, the duration) of a single beat is expressed as a *quarter note*. All other notes are expressed in relation to this value and may be thought of in terms of fractions. A note half as long as quarter note is therefore called an *eighth note*; another way to express the same idea is that two eighth notes equal one quarter note. In TAB, quarter notes are notated with a vertical line called a *stem* that descends from the number on the staff; single eighth notes add a *flag* to the stem, while eighth notes in groups are joined by a heavy line called a *beam*.

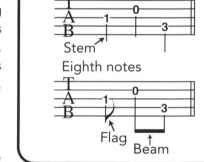

Time Signatures
The time value of each measure is expressed by a *time signature*. The top number of any time signature tells you the number of beats in each measure. The bottom number tells you which value is equal to one beat; a "4" on the bottom indicates a quarter note is equal to one beat, and an "8" indicates that an eighth note is equal to one beat.

All four measures in the example below contain two beats, each indicated by a slash mark (/). Clap along as you count the beats for each measure out loud.

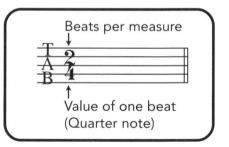

Chapter 2

Starting to Play

Using the Left Hand

Most of the time, you'll hold the banjo by using your left hand to cradle the neck around the first few frets. (Note: If you're left-handed, you can reverse the instructions in this book as necessary.) The neck will rest in the crook between your thumb and other fingers. The goal is to create a fairly straight line from hand to elbow without bending at the wrist. This will cause the least amount of tension.

Rest the banjo between the thumb and fingers. The wrist should be straight.

One of the most important principles to keep in mind in using *both* hands is *economy of motion*. This involves moving your hands as little as possible, which will help you play cleanly at faster speeds as well as develop a more refined touch. Keep your fingers fairly close to the fingerboard. There will be times when your fingers will resist coming down; don't make yourself crazy trying to discipline them, but make economy of motion one of your primary goals. In banjo playing, the fingers of your left hand are numbered as shown in the photo at right.

Avoid tensing your left hand, which is a common problem when learning a new chord. Tension will make it harder to form the chord, and it may also cause you to *choke* (laterally bend) the strings, which will in turn make you play out of tune. If this happens, let go of the neck, shake out your hand, and try it again. Left-hand tension can be hard to remedy, even when you're aware of it. Fretting properly is one of the best ways of avoiding left-hand tension. Fret notes just on the nut side of the fret itself. Don't fret in the middle of the spaces between frets, and don't press your left-hand fingers down any harder than is necessary to achieve a clean sound.

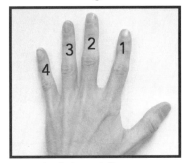

Left-hand fingers

Chords

Now you're almost ready to play some music. First, though, you need to become familiar with *chords*. A chord is a group of three (or more) notes played simultaneously.

Use your thumb to strum an open G chord (all five strings open) for each of the marked beats in the example below. Make sure that all the strums are evenly spaced in time. (Note: In all examples, the chord does not change until a new chord symbol appears above the staff.)

Track 2

The D7 Chord

Let's open things up a bit and learn another chord: D7. This time, your left hand will get in on the action. You'll need your 1st and 2nd fingers for the D7 chord. Strum only the first four strings, since the short 5th string (G) isn't part of the chord.

3

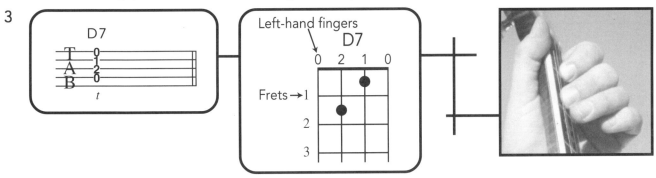

As you're fretting the D7 or any other chord, be sure that you're almost touching the next highest fret. This will help you get a good, clean sound. If you're too close to the next lowest fret, your strings will buzz. Try it yourself so that you'll see (and hear) what to avoid.

When learning a new chord, it's best to first strum it slowly, one string at a time (starting with the highest-numbered string), to make sure that every note rings clearly. When fingering a chord, be sure not to let your fingers touch adjacent strings, which will result in a damping effect.

Now, let's combine the D7 and G chords:

Here's an old song that the folk group the Weavers used to play. Remember to maintain an even space between strums.

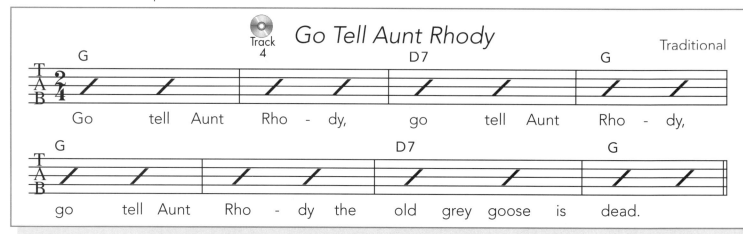

Go Tell Aunt Rhody

Traditional

Go tell Aunt Rho - dy, go tell Aunt Rho - dy,

go tell Aunt Rho - dy the old grey goose is dead.

Tom Dooley, a 19th-century ballad that recounts the true story of a man who went to the gallows to save the life of his lover, Ann Melton, became an unexpected hit when the Kingston Trio included it on their 1958 debut album.

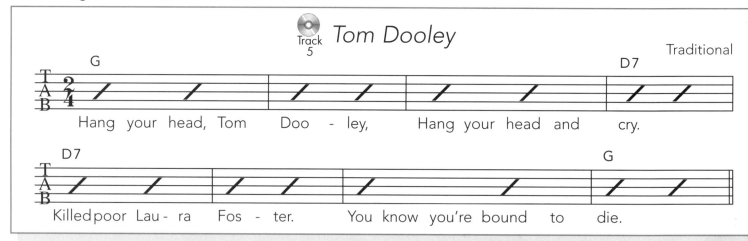

Tom Dooley

Traditional

Hang your head, Tom Doo - ley, Hang your head and cry.

Killed poor Lau - ra Fos - ter. You know you're bound to die.

The C Chord

The C chord completes the all-important triumvirate of G, D7 and C. With these three chords you'll be able to play literally tens of thousands of songs.

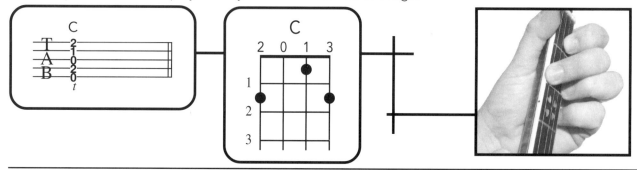

If you find it too difficult to fret the 4th string at the 2nd fret, leave it out for now and just strum the first three strings—but keep working to get that 4th string in there. Here's an exercise that will get you going back and forth between G and C:

The following exercise adds D7. Keep the left-hand index finger on the second string, first fret while changing from C to D7.

BANJO BUILDER: DOWNBEATS AND PICKUPS

All the examples you've played so far have begun on the first beat of a measure (also called the *downbeat*), which is normally the strongest beat. Many tunes, however, begin partway through a measure, which means that the first downbeat occurs in the following measure. This partial measure at the beginning of a tune that leads to the first downbeat is called a *pickup measure* or just a *pickup*.

Think of downbeats and pickups in terms of how some words are pronounced. Downbeats are like words whose accents fall on the first syllable (for example, "banjo," "bluegrass" or "music"). Pickups are like words that gather steam on the first syllable, leading to an accent on the second (for example, "applause," "achieve" or "success").

In the next tune, *Michael, Row the Boat Ashore*, the first downbeat occurs on "row," which is also where you play the first chord. (In many tunes there is no chord in the pickup measure.) "Michael," the pickup, actually falls on beat 2 of an incomplete measure.

Enjoy this longtime folk favorite, which will help you navigate between G, C and D7.

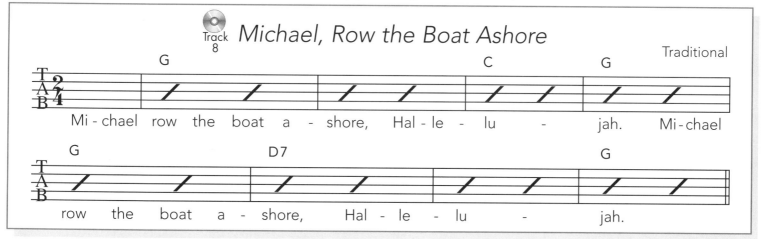

Here's one more song to strum that we'll later explore in more detail:

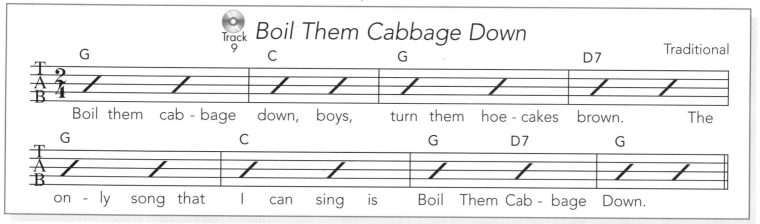

Chapter 3

Using the Right Hand

Now we'll prepare to pick. In banjo playing, the right hand is where all the action is—not just in terms of flash, but also in solidity and overall tone production. (Again, if you play left-handed, just flip things around, as necessary.)

Much of your sense of musical timing will come from your right hand. Good rhythm is the most important thing you can have as a banjo player. (See Chapter 4 for a detailed discussion of time and rhythm.) The right hand is also largely responsible for the particular quality of your tone. If you play right next to the bridge, you'll have a crisp edge, a sound associated with bluegrass legend Ralph Stanley. If you move away from the bridge an inch or more, you'll get a more mellow sound that is suitable for some fiddle music, various kinds of backup, or plain old pretty tunes.

One of the most important things that will affect your tone is how you actually strike the strings. Your goal should be to find a balance between hitting the strings too hard—sacrificing tone for noise and giving ammunition to the instrument's detractors—and too softly, which results in lackluster projection. Some players live in apartments with thin walls or have relationships on the brink, and a loud banjo might lead to a night in the bus station. Some have tackled the volume problem by stuffing T-shirts in their resonators or using a banjo mute.

Playing too hard can also create tension in the right hand, which makes it difficult to play cleanly. A tense right hand will likely result in missed notes and an inability to play fast (or at least fast *and* accurately). Your right-hand approach will also depend on the kind of music you're playing. This book deals mostly with a straight-ahead bluegrass style in which you want a fairly strong sound. When I play classical music, fiddle tunes or sweeter, progressive tunes, I lay back a little bit. Keep these things in mind and be open to changing your playing according to what is appropriate to the style and context.

As you might have gathered, there is no one correct way to hold your right hand. Start with a position that feels comfortable. Just bring your arm across the arm rest (if you have one), or across the stretcher band and brackets, and let your hand fall naturally across the strings. (See page 4 for a photo that shows the various parts of the instrument.) Try to achieve a certain amount of arch in your wrist—not enough to neccesitate an emergency call to the chiropractor, but enough to have you lording over the strings a bit; use the first photo below as a guideline. This will give you a bigger, richer sound and minimize the chances of hitting the head with your picks. Do *not* allow the bottom of your wrist to hit the head, as in the second photo below.

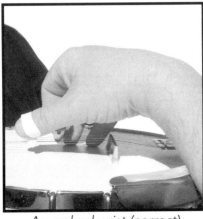

An arched wrist (correct)

A flat wrist (incorrect)

Your right pinkie or ring finger (or both) can rest on the head as you play. Some players insist that you should keep two fingers on the head in order to provide the strongest anchor while *t, i* and *m* churn away on *Foggy Mountain Breakdown*. I've seen beginning pickers spend a week with their ring and pinkie fingers bound with rubber bands to keep them together.

The characteristics of the tendons and muscles in every player's hands vary somewhat, and sometimes the ring finger will want to move along with the middle finger. If your hand works this way, don't worry. Earl Scruggs has almost always kept two fingers on the head, and as a result, this has become the standard way of playing. As long as at least one finger (ring or pinkie) is planted, you'll be in good shape.

For playing straight-ahead bluegrass, it's a good idea to place your pinkie close to the bridge without actually touching it. This will give you a good "crack" when you're wailing on a hardscrabble instrumental. Try not to touch the bridge. Since the bridge transmits the vibrations of the strings to the body of the instrument, touching the bridge (and stopping the vibrations) will produce a muting effect. The sound will become a bit quieter and lose its brilliance. Take care to keep the sound open.

From time to time, people ask me which hand to look at while playing. Initially you may have a hard time plucking the correct string, and you may feel compelled to stare at the right hand to ensure accuracy. This is particularly true when you first use picks. As you gain confidence and experience, you should watch your left hand to make sure you're moving to the correct fret, especially when playing up the neck. The right hand should take care of itself within a short time.

Picks

Some players worry about the "Edward Scissorhands" effect when it comes to using picks; however, picks are the final element you'll need as you progress toward a real bluegrass sound on the banjo. For bluegrass playing, you'll want to use a plastic or metal thumb pick on *t*, and metal finger picks on *i* and *m*. Picks are crucial when playing in a four- or five-piece band; they give you the extra volume needed to cut through the sounds of the other instruments.

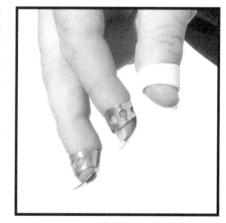

I suggest you use picks throughout this book. However, I've had students who really did not want to use picks, and many fabulous old-time musicians have played beautiful banjo music without picks. If you're just playing by yourself, it doesn't make much of a difference. But if you want to kick into *Foggy Mountain Breakdown* with that strong, deep, rich, clear swirl of sound that Earl Scruggs has, you'll need to use picks.

The picks you use should be tight enough to stay on your fingers while playing, but not so tight that they cut off circulation in your fingertips. They should be thin enough to bend into a comfortable shape, but not so thin that they feel flimsy. I use Dunlop .020 gauge picks, which work nicely on all counts. I used to put my picks on just as they came from the store, rather than shaping them in a particular way; I would just push them together on both sides to get them to grip my fingers. More recently, I've pushed the picks up on the front so that they would more closely follow the contour of my fingers. Earl Scruggs, Béla Fleck, Pete Wernick and other players do this. Some players use picks that are bent almost straight out. Experiment to see what works for you. The picks I use are shown in the photos at right.

Here are some picking tips to remember:
1. As you pick, you thumb should move down (toward you fingers).
2. Your fingers should move up, toward your palm.
3. Play near the tips of the picks. (See the "Banjo Builder" on page 30 for more tips on using picks.)

Playing in 4/4 Time

As we approach the Foothills of·Earl Scruggs, we'll use quarter notes as a transition from strumming to playing rolls. So far, you've played in 2/4 (two quarter notes per measure). Now, you'll play in 4/4 (four quarter notes per measure).

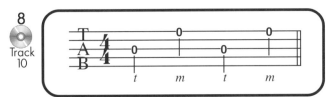

The Pinch

In banjo playing, a *pinch* describes the motion of your fingers playing two strings, and thus two notes, at the same time. In the next exercise, try alternating the 3rd string (*t*) with a simultaneous pinch on the 2nd string (*i*) and 1st string (*m*).

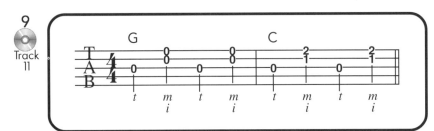

The extraordinary songwriter (Gentle on My Mind), banjoist, fiddler, riverboater and dancer **John Hartford** *was a beloved and hugely influential musician. His passing in 2001 was a profound loss to the acoustic music community.*

Next, move *t* from the 3rd string to the 4th, then to the 5th and back to the 4th.
Alternate each *t* move with a pinch as shown below.

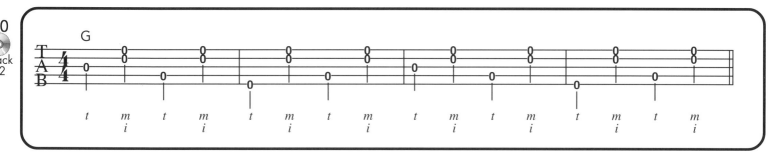

Here's an exercise, adapted from a century-old instructional book by Otto Albrecht,
that adds the D7. Try it; you'll be playing real instrumental music!

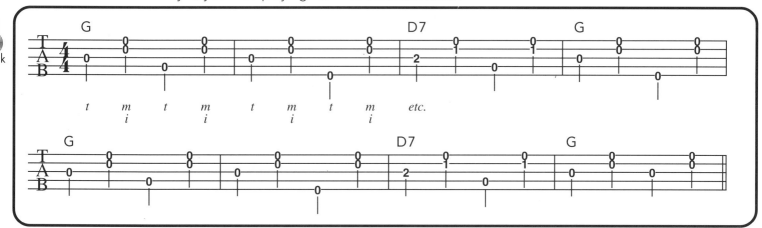

Boil Them Cabbage Down is well suited to a similar treatment. In the second-to-last measure, be sure to fret the full D7 chord, even though only the 2nd string is marked in the TAB. There are no hard and fast rules about this in TAB, but I generally finger the full chord wherever a chord is indicated, even if not all the notes are called for in the notation. The unplayed "extra" strings will vibrate lightly—sympathetically with the others—giving you a fuller sound, which is especially pleasing when you play by yourself; (Note: Lyrics normally appear below the TAB, but in some examples in this book, they appear above to avoid collision with the right-hand fingerings.)

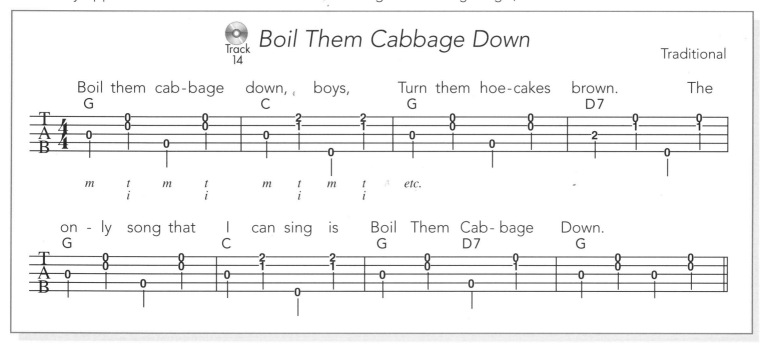

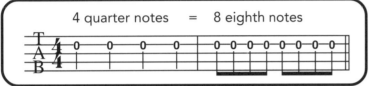

Rolls and Melody

Rolls are right-hand finger patterns that are the building blocks of bluegrass banjo. Rolls generally use eighth-note rhythms. By now, you're used to playing four quarter notes per measure, which is equivalent to twice as many eighth notes. This rhythmic pattern of eight eighth notes, notated as two groups of four, is standard for bluegrass-style rolls.

12

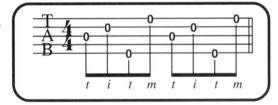

The Square Roll

Here's an example of an extremely handy four-note roll sometimes called a *titm* or a *thumb-in-and-out roll*. I refer to the *titm* as a *square roll*, because two of them fit squarely into one measure.

13

Here are four measures of the square roll using the open G chord:

14

Track 15

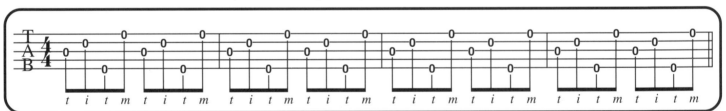

Notice in Example 14 above that we never use the same right-hand finger on consecutive eighth notes. At slow speeds this makes no difference. At faster speeds, however, having to play two eighth notes in a row with the same finger will slow you down and cause the tempo to drag. In this book, all fingerings are provided; when you begin to make arrangements of your own, you'll want to keep in mind this principle of using different fingers for consecutive notes. There are some cases in which players will "double up" on a finger, but these are fairly rare.

This version of *Go Tell Aunt Rhody* applies the square roll to chords you already know.

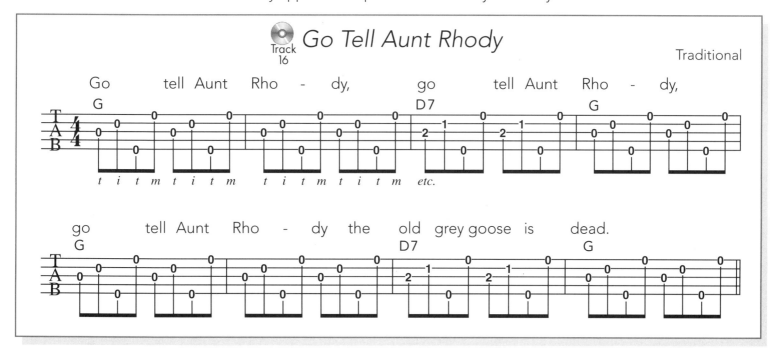

Try the same pattern with *It Ain't Gonna Rain No More.*

BANJO MASTERS SPEAK: Pete Wernick

"Before learning banjo solos, learn how to change chords smoothly and keep time with a simple rhythm strum. This is important groundwork for soloing and for playing with others. Use a songbook and sing or hum through easy, familiar songs. When that's going well, change to a simple titm roll instead of the strum. Once you can do this, you can have hours of fun at a 'slowjam.'

"To learn soloing, start with a few easy TABs, then try to find melodies by ear and make up your own solos. Stay with it. If you love it enough to try hard and be patient, you'll get it."

Melody

As we begin to concentrate on melody, here are a few important points to consider. Melody is the key to any song; often, the melody *is* the song. Focus on bringing out the melody as you play, rather than just producing a hail of notes. This is especially important when you're taking the opening solo on a song, since an audience will want to be able to recognize a tune from the start. As you become more proficient, you may be tempted to go a little overboard with hot licks. If you're trying out something new, playing around the house or just having some fun, there's no reason not to. But in the end, to paraphrase John Hartford, playing is about the tune, not about the player. Honor the melody and play it as truly as you can. There's real beauty in that. Making the melody sing can be a little tricky when you're first approaching a tune, especially at a slow speed; still, as you're learning, be sure to play each of the melody notes with a bit of emphasis so that each is absolutely clear.

Let's look at *Boil Them Cabbage Down* in terms of melody. First, try playing it using square rolls.

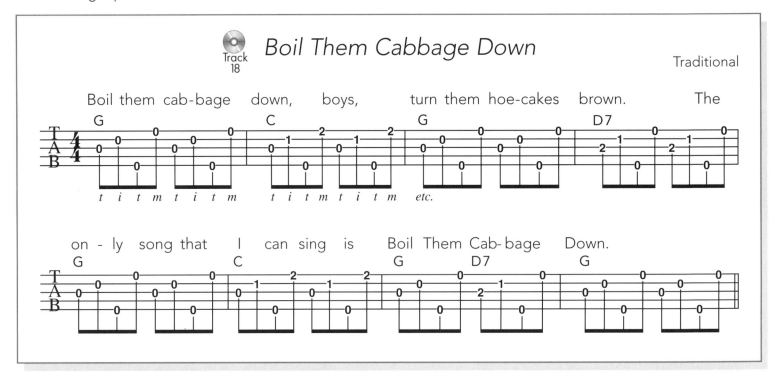

BANJO MASTERS SPEAK: Bill Keith

"The five-string banjo is a great instrument, and the more you learn, the more fun you'll have playing it. When you're getting started, it's really important to establish a solid foundation. Playing along with other musicians or with recordings will be a big help. Above all, enjoy!"

BANJO MASTERS SPEAK:
Alison Brown

"I started playing banjo when I was ten, and for the first couple of years, I found it much more difficult than playing guitar (my first instrument). Getting used to playing with picks on my fingers was the biggest obstacle. Even now, I only have one set of picks that I feel really comfortable with. But the good news is that if you stick with it, it will get easier— I promise. Pick it solid!"

*In the 1990s, **Alison Brown** played and recorded with Alison Krauss's Union Station and has since toured with her own quartet. Brown's bluegrass- and jazz-influenced albums on the Compass label are a must-have.*

C Chord (Alternate Version)

The next version of *Boil Them Cabbage Down* uses a pretty version of the C chord. You'll finger it like this:

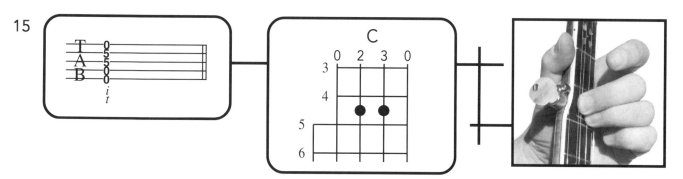

Notice in the arrangement at the top of page 18 that the melody is integrated into the square roll and that no matter how the melody moves, the square roll remains a constant presence in the background. The square roll, in fact, can be put to good use in almost any tune in which the melody notes fall on the 3rd or 4th strings. As you play, use *t* for all the melody notes, and keep the 2nd finger of your left hand on the 3rd string at all times. Here and in the rest of the book, melody notes are highlighted in grey for easy identification.

Boil Them Cabbage Down

Traditional

■ = Melody note

Let's try the square roll with *Go Tell Aunt Rhody*. Here we'll use a variation on the square roll that requires only the first three strings.

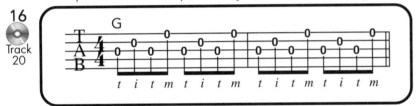

Now, integrate this variation with the square roll you've already used.

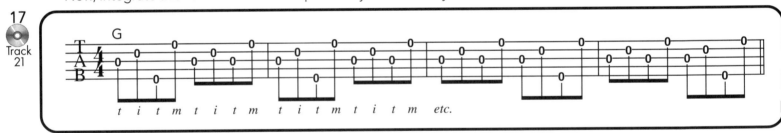

For this arrangement of *Go Tell Aunt Rhody*, you'll use your left-hand 2nd finger on the 3rd string as you just did for *Boil Them Cabbage Down*. Notice that the melody sometimes moves from one note to the next in the middle of a square roll.

Go Tell Aunt Rhody

Traditional

BANJO BUILDER: MEMORIZATION

Now that you have a couple of songs under your belt, think about memorizing them. Avoid becoming a "TAB junkie"—one of those players who's hard-pressed to play the tunes he or she knows without using the written-out music as a safety net. Some players need to make a deliberate effort to memorize music; others find that after playing a tune a number of times, it just sticks in their heads and their fingers. Everyone learns differently and at a different pace, but memorizing the tunes you know—correctly—is a step on the road to *really* making the music yours.

Once you're comfortable with the TAB for a tune, close the book to see how much of the tune you can play from memory. You may have to peek at the music once in a while, but make a conscious effort to wean yourself from the printed page. Once you're confident that you've memorized a tune, go back to the TAB to make sure that every note and chord is correct. One consequence of learning mistakes is that you'll eventually have to unlearn them—which is much less fun than making music.

The Forward-Backward Roll

The *forward-backward roll* is another essential finger pattern. As the name implies, it's made up of two separate rolls. The *forward roll* uses the thumb, index finger and middle finger, in that order, on any three strings. Here's an example of a forward roll.

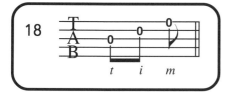

The *backward roll* uses the same fingers in the opposite order.

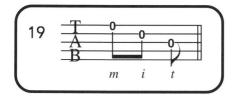

Later, we'll look at forward and backward rolls individually. First, though, we'll combine them in a forward-backward roll, since two of these rolls fit squarely into a measure.

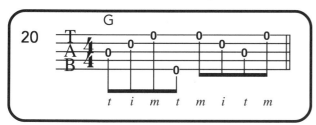

Notice that the above example begins with a forward roll, moves to the 5th string (which acts as a pivot) and goes into the backward roll, finishing off with a beautiful dismount on the 1st string. The judges give it a 5.6.

Like the square roll, the forward-backward roll is useful when you want to place the melody on the 3rd and 4th strings. Your solos will become more interesting when you start combining the rolls. Try this arrangement of *Boil Them Cabbage Down* that uses the square roll and adds the forward-backward roll on the C and D7 chords.

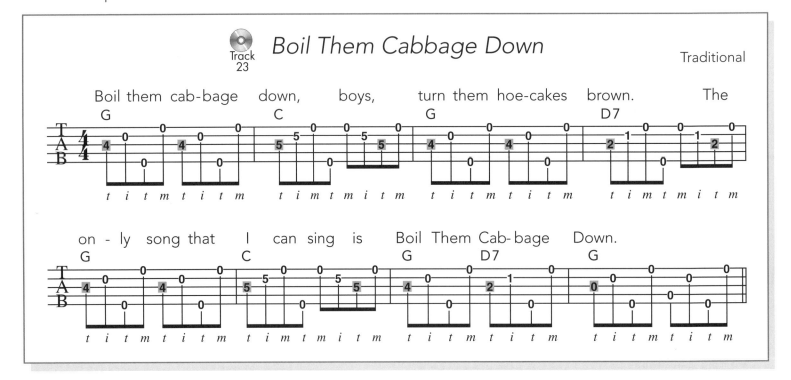

Try these variations on the forward-backward roll.

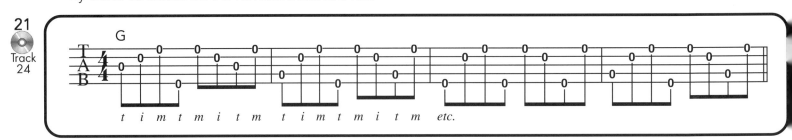

Now use these variations with G, C and D7 chords. The C chord in the second measure of this example includes an open 1st string. This *shorthand* C, used frequently by top players, sweetens the chord with a bit of extra resonance.

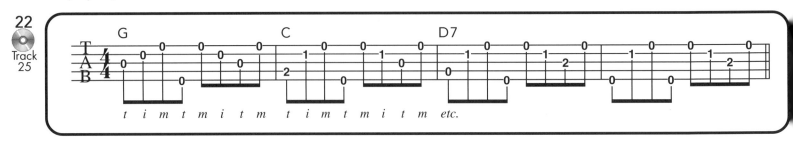

She'll Be Comin' 'Round the Mountain works nicely with a combination of square and forward-backward rolls. Start by evenly strumming two chords per measure before you pick the tune. This will allow you to first familarize yourself with the chords, which is a good way to approach every new tune you learn. Notice that the song begins with a pickup of four eighth notes (i.e., one square roll).

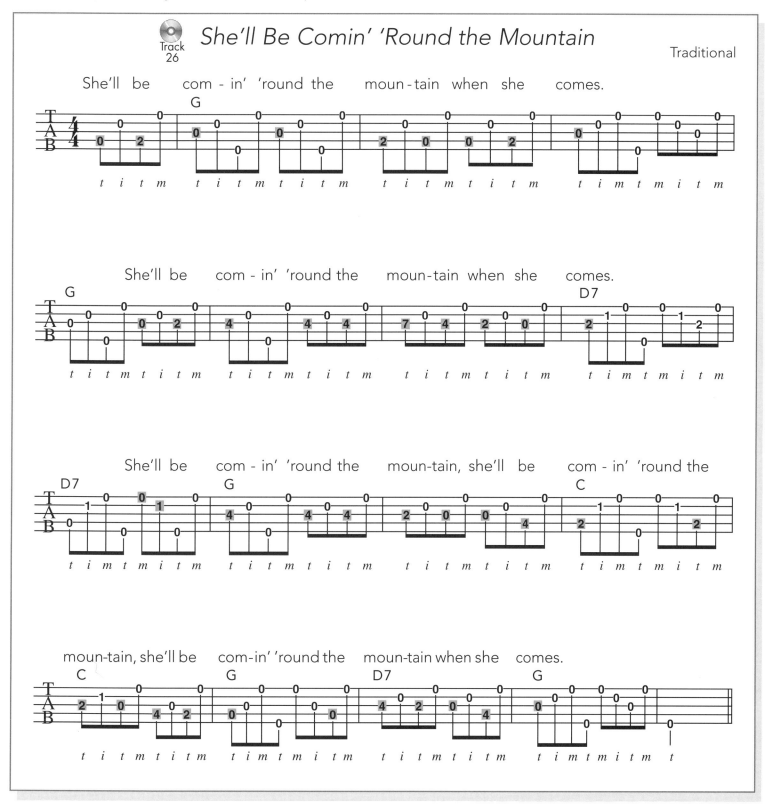

She'll Be Comin' 'Round the Mountain

Track 26

Traditional

BANJO BUILDER: STRONG ON THE STRINGS

Make sure every note you play is strong and crystal clear. Many players don't sound certain strings as loudly as they should; it might be the 5th or the 2nd string that's a bit too quiet, but most often it's the 1st string that's on the verge of inaudibility. A strong *m* technique on the 1st string adds rhythmic punch and a professional edge to your playing. Listen to Earl Scruggs, J. D. Crowe or Béla Fleck: You'll hear every note they play very clearly. It's easy to backslide and forget that you need to bring out a particular note or string. Practice eternal vigilance.

The Forward Roll

With the forward roll, you'll dramatically enrich the playing possibilities of your right hand. The forward roll is a key element in bluegrass banjo, and one that helps drive the music. It's particularly handy when you want to play fast, and it's also effective in bringing out melody notes on the 3rd and 4th strings.

As explained earlier, the forward roll is a three-note roll that uses, in order, the right thumb, index and middle fingers. Try these four different forward rolls.

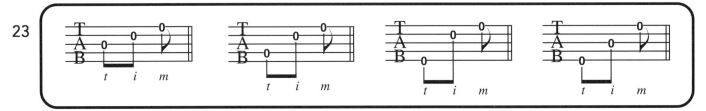

Because forward rolls contain three notes, they can't be used on their own to neatly fill out a measure of eight eighth notes. (By contrast, two square rolls or one forward-backward roll fit snugly into a measure.) So, if you want to use consecutive forward rolls, it's necessary to fill out the measure with two additional eighth notes. In the example below, "extra" notes are placed together at the ends of the measures.

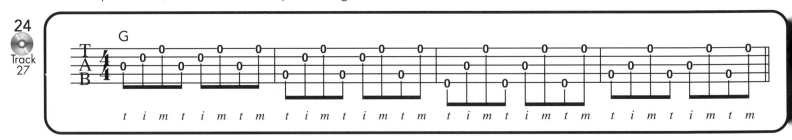

Here, we'll use the forward roll with two other chords, C and D7, and put the "extra" notes at the beginning of each measure.

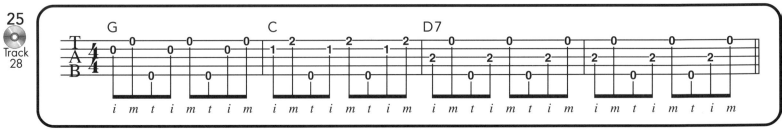

BANJO BUILDER: REPEAT SIGNS

Before we get to *Banks of the Ohio,* you'll need to know something about *repeat signs.* Most fiddle tunes and many other tunes are made up of two parts, each of which is repeated. To save space and make reading easier, such passages are often marked with repeat signs:

Repeat signs indicate that you'll repeat as a unit all the musical material that occurs between them. In *Banks of the Ohio,* you'll play the tune all the way through, go back to the repeat sign near the beginning, and play from there to the end. If a song or section repeats from the very beginning of the first measure, the first repeat sign is usually omitted. The number of times you'll cycle through this process depends on the number of verses—or simply how many times you want to play the tune.

Banks of the Ohio is a beautiful old-time tune that lends itself well to the forward roll.
In this case, each series of forward rolls spins off from a single melody note.

The G7 Chord

The next example using the forward roll includes a new chord, G7, a transitional chord that leads you from G to C. Use your 2nd finger on the 3rd fret of the 4th string, as shown below.

26

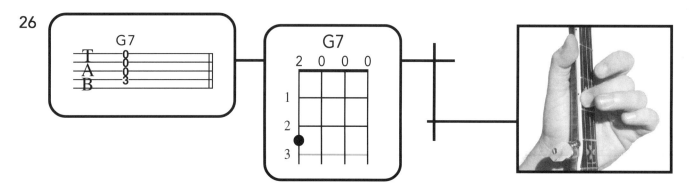

In the last measure of the next exercise, you can fret the descending 5–4–2 line on the 3rd string with your left 2nd finger. You will achieve greater economy of motion, however, by using your 4th finger for the 5, the 3rd finger for the 4 and the 1st finger for the 2. Note that the 2nd finger, which would ordinarily take the 3rd fret, isn't used here.

27 Track 30

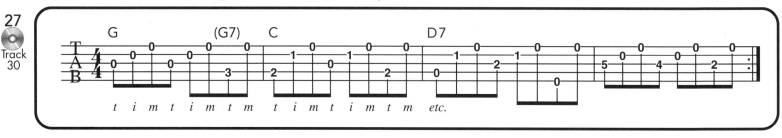

Handsome Molly is one of my favorite tunes. The first version you'll learn uses mostly square and forward-backward rolls.

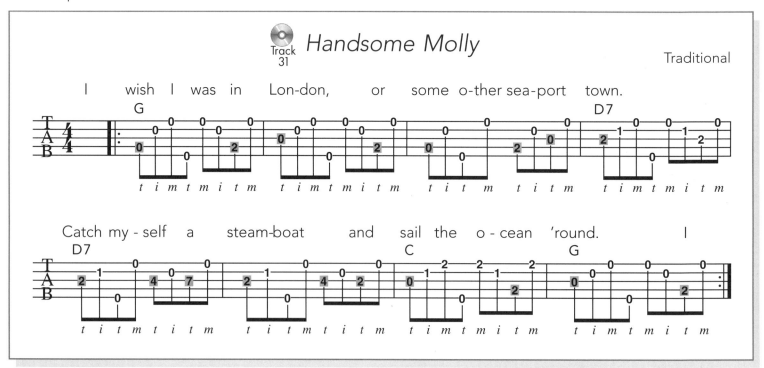

Track 31 *Handsome Molly*

Traditional

I wish I was in Lon-don, or some o-ther sea-port town.

Catch my - self a steam-boat and sail the o - cean 'round. I

Now try it with a combination of forward and forward-backward rolls:

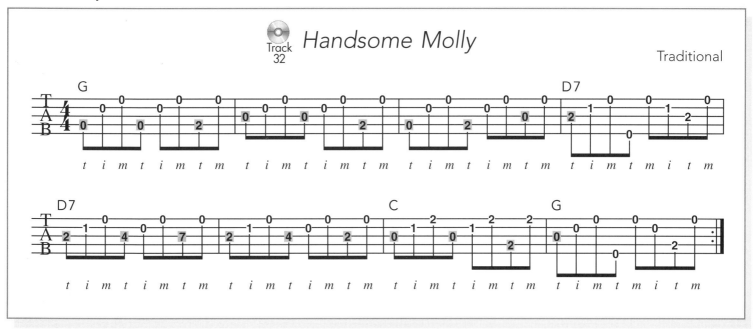

BANJO BUILDER: SYNCOPATION

The above version of *Handsome Molly* has a much different, almost Caribbean, feel. This sense of imbalance, which results from the stacking of forward rolls, is called *syncopation*. In simplest terms, syncopation is a shifting of accents from strong to weak beats. In most of the examples you've played so far, rhythmic accents occur on each strong beat (falling on the first and fifth eighth notes in the measure). Think of a measure that begins with two forward rolls. Since each forward roll contains three notes, the beginning of the second roll occurs an eighth note early (on the fourth eighth note of the measure) in relation to the strong beat. This "hiccup" that adds a little zip to the rhythmic feel is syncopation.

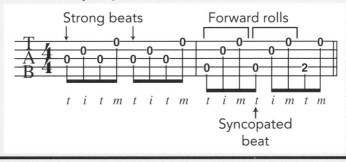

Now that you have a small arsenal of different roll patterns at your disposal, try combining rolls in the tunes you learn as I did in the two versions of *Handsome Molly*. This can be an effective way to bring your own personality into the music. Don't be afraid to spend some time away from the printed page.

The Backward Roll

The backward roll, as you have already seen, reverses the direction of the forward roll. It is especially effective for placing the melody on the 1st string.

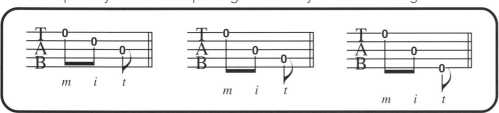

Like forward rolls, backward rolls can be stacked in sequence. For now, let's use the backward roll as part of a practical but largely unheralded application.

The Backward-Forward Roll

I love the backward-forward roll. It's basically a forward-backward roll cut in two and put back together with the two halves switched.

29

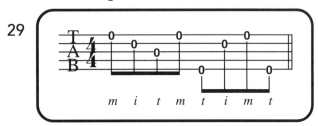

Rock on with the backward-forward roll in this next example. Here you'll use a different version of G7 in which you fret the 3rd fret of the 1st string with your 4th finger.

30

Track 33

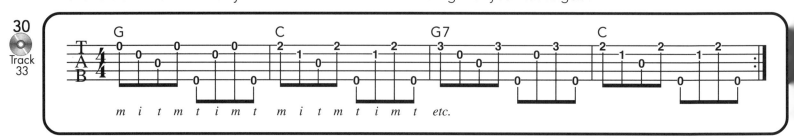

For more applications of the backward-forward roll, look at the first two lines of *Old Joe Clark* on page 28.

Using Quarter Notes

It's time to integrate quarter notes into the patterns you've learned. (See page 6 for a review of quarter notes.) Remember that quarter notes have twice the value of eighth notes, so a measure of four quarters equals a measure of eight eighths. Here's a quarter-note exercise that you can use as the basis for an ending to a bluegrass solo:

31

Track 34

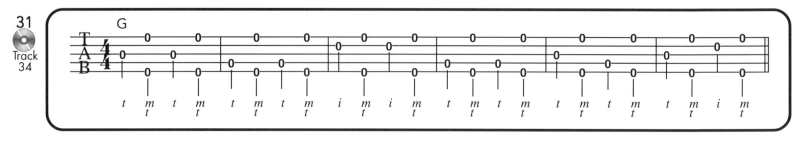

Let's mix in eighth notes by adding a square roll:

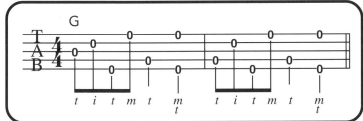

Though we started with eighth-note rolls to ease you into bluegrass playing, you'll now learn how to integrate quarter notes into your roll patterns. Earl Scruggs, for example, does this to accentuate particular melody notes; sometimes he'll play four melody notes in a row as quarter notes. Let's try combining quarter notes with a different kind of roll.

The Minstrel Roll

I call this roll the *minstrel roll* because it gives you the same notes, though in a different style, as a figure common in minstrel (African-American-influenced music performed by whites in blackface) banjo music of the mid-19th century.

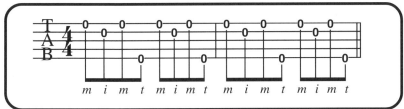

BANJO BUILDER: PHRASING

One advantage of adding quarter notes to your solos is that their greater length allows tunes to breathe. Singers and wind players have to stop to take a breath once in a while. This helps create *phrasing*, the feeling of ending one musical "sentence" and beginning another.

The minstrel roll is well suited to the bluegrass favorite *Old Joe Clark*. Below is the basic melody in quarter notes. Use your 1st finger on the 1st fret of the 2nd string and the 2nd fret of the 1st string, and your 2nd finger for the 3rd fret of the 1st string.

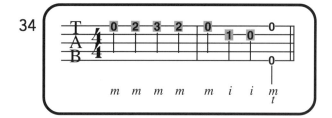

Enjoy this great standard!

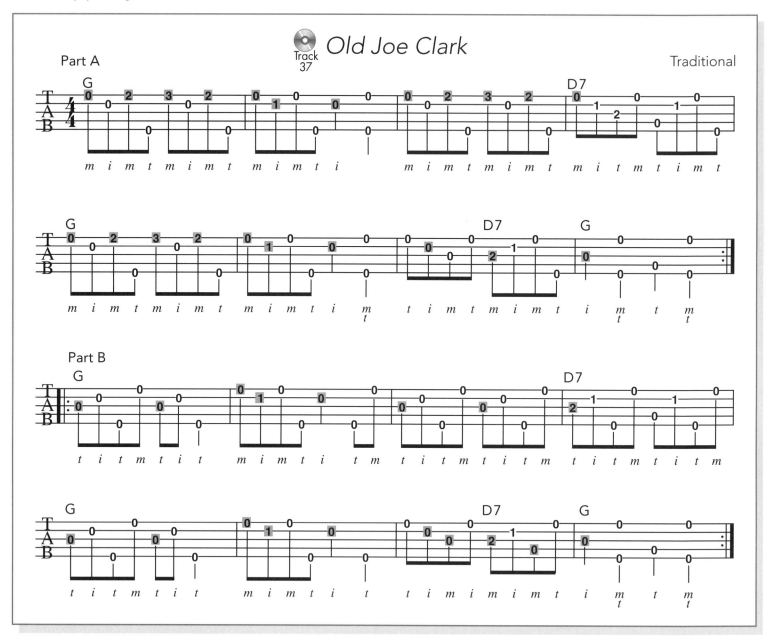

One of my favorite old-time fiddle tunes is *Cluck Old Hen.* Here's a minstrel-roll version based on the playing of the wonderful North Carolina fiddler Tommy Jarrell and his sometime partner, Fred Cockerham. Use your right index finger on the 3rd (instead of the 2nd) string, as shown in Example 35.

35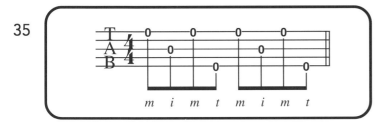

Cluck Old Hen includes an F chord, which also appears in many other old-time and bluegrass tunes. Here's how to fret it:

36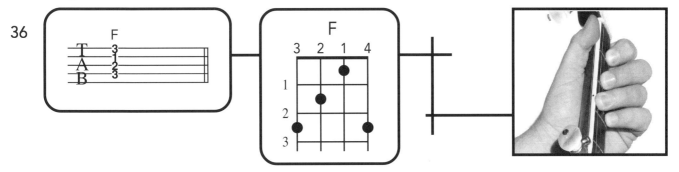

You may find the F chord a bit of a stretch for your left hand, but in this version of *Cluck Old Hen* you can leave the 1st string open when you play the chord. This will give you a simple D7 position with the addition of the 3rd finger on the 4th string, 3rd fret. Don't forget to heed the repeat signs; both part A and part B are repeated.

Did you notice the forward-backward rolls in the B section? The first one begins half-way through the first measure and finishes in the first half of the following measure. This use of the roll is known as *crossing bar lines.*

BANJO BUILDER: (NOT) HITTING THE HEAD

Let's take a break from playing to talk about an issue that will have a big impact on your sound. Pick noise is something that many people are unconscious of when playing, but it is another important detail you need to keep high on your playing checklist. This common problem occurs when you allow one or more of your right-hand fingers to hit against the head as you pick.

There are a number of ways to deal with this problem. Consider the common-sense wisdom of the old joke:

> Patient: Doctor, every time I do this with my arm it hurts.
> Doctor: Don't do that.

That's how I used to approach the problem of pick noise with my students—I would instruct them, in short, to self-consciously watch their right hands and not allow their fingers to go down far enough to hit the head. Ian Perry, a wonderful Canadian banjoist and instructor, once shared his perspective. He suggested an exercise that begins with having your fingers poised just above the strings. Start "picking" without actually hitting the strings. Then, lower your fingers to the strings so they're barely making contact and producing sound. Look at your fingers to see how high up they are. With time and repetition, you'll instinctively adjust to the correct height.

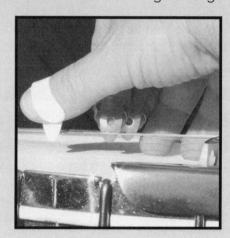

A good way to observe the position of your fingers in relation to the strings is to turn your banjo in such a way that the strings merge in your line of vision, then start to pick. This will give you the clearest view of the problem area.

BANJO MASTERS SPEAK: Béla Fleck

"It's good to play stuff that you really like because it'll make you want to play more. You'll make a lot of progress if you're excited to get the banjo into your hands."

Béla Fleck (right), a musician of astounding abilities, has been more influential than any other banjoist of his generation in bringing the instrument to a wider audience. Since the early 1990s, he has toured regularly with his groundbreaking group, the Flecktones (Victor Wooten, left; Futureman, center).

Chapter 5

All in the Timing

"Timing's the most important thing. It's all in the timing."—**John Hartford**

John Hartford, composer of *Gentle on My Mind* and many other songs and instrumentals, was a fantastic banjo player, fiddler and calligrapher—and his quote above is right on target. John had a compelling right-hand groove that got right inside you and made you want to move. In fact, he used to lay a plywood board with a pickup on the stage and dance on it while he played and sang.

Rhythm should be the primary driving force of the music you play. As your skills increase and you learn some hot licks and fancy runs, you may have a tendency to concentrate more on left-hand fingerings than on keeping a steady rhythm with the right hand. No matter what is going on in the left hand, it should always defer to the right.

One story has Flatt and Scruggs standing in front of a house picking a tune, walking around the house in opposite directions and meeting back in front, still in time with each other. Whether fact or legend, it certainly makes a point about having a rock-solid sense of rhythm and timing.

Using a Metronome

A surefire way to improve your sense of musical time is to play along with a metronome. You can get a perfectly adequate metronome for about 30 dollars. I recommend a portable, battery-operated one that is easy to carry around. Most metronomes of this type include a light that flashes in time with the click, giving you both visual and aural cues to keep your fingers in sync.

Some people prefer to use a drum machine in place of a metronome. Pete Wernick uses one, and you can usually get more volume from a drum machine than from a metronome. Drum machines also have the advantage of being programmable, which means you can change the feel of the groove. If you can't hear the click, play more quietly.

Playing along with CDs can help your timing to a certain extent; however, if you're playing along with four or five musicians, it can be difficult to hear the exact point at which to place the beat. With a metronome or drum machine, it's just you and the click; there's no hiding from the rhythm.

Some people have trouble locking in with the click. Here are some suggestions for making effective use of a metronome in your practice routine. Start by playing slowly. You'll get a good idea of your sense of timing when there are larger spaces between the clicks. Set the metronome at a rate anywhere between 60 and 72 (metronome markings refer to the number of clicks per minute). Play two notes per click. I find that one note per click doesn't allow the music to breathe, while four notes per click allows more space for you to waver in your timing. At first, just play open rolls so that you don't need to worry about the left hand. Just concentrate on the right hand.

The marks above the staff at right indicate where the metronome clicks fall. Notice in this example that you need to have your right thumb lock in with the click. Though I've indicated only two rolls, you should repeat this exercise for at least a minute or two.

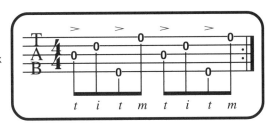

As you become more comfortable working with the metronome, you can vary the placement of the clicks so that they fall on the second, fourth, sixth and eighth notes of the measure, which will give you a *backbeat*.

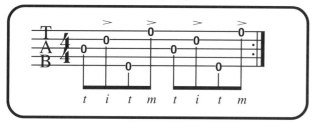

Building Up Speed

As a bluegrass banjo player, speed is an issue you will need to deal with sooner or later. Some folks are born with the ability to play fast as greased lightning; others have to work at it. I had a student some years ago who was diligent in learning his playing assignments. He would hit the notes perfectly but could never progress beyond a slow roll. After a few months of teaching him, I felt we needed to work on his speed. First, I set the metronome at the fastest tempo—which wasn't very fast—at which he could play the tune cleanly. Then I moved the tempo up one notch, he played the tune again, and we kept repeating this cycle. This process of gradually increasing the tempo continued for a good half hour. By the end of the lesson, the student had doubled his speed. I can't guarantee this result for everyone, but give it a shot. Try using the metronome in this way to build up speed on the exercises you've already played.

PHOTO • DON FISHER

*After a stint with Jimmy Martin, **Alan Munde** founded Country Gazette with Byron Berline. His picking, both traditional and progressive, has inspired countless players.*

BANJO MASTERS SPEAK: Alan Munde

"Groove is very important in music and to the musicians in an ensemble setting. Certainly the bands of Bill Monroe, Flatt and Scruggs, and Jimmy Martin, and many of the current groups, connect with the groove. It is that feeling of fluid, frictionless togetherness that comes from recognizing the importance of the beat— each note of the banjo roll connecting with the rhythm of the other instruments in the ensemble as they, in turn, are connected to the cosmic metronome set in motion at the beginning of the number.

"There are many ways to start working towards that sense of groove and participate in the music, even if you are a beginner and don't know how to play songs yet. Damp the strings with your left hand, so the sound you get is a pitchless click. Relax, close your eyes and pick along as best you can with a metronome, or better, your favorite recording, using a simple roll or an even simpler rhythm vamp—anything percussive— until you feel yourself "in" with the pulse of the music. This will help you to begin to get that groove into your fingers and head. Do this until you gain the skills to actually play along."

> **BANJO MASTERS SPEAK:** *Tom Adams*
>
> *"It's not about tone rings and bridges and certain brands of capos. It's about you focusing your mind and your passion, and putting in the time with your banjo actually in your hands practicing. Practice now. Think about the banjo now. You learn to play the banjo by actually playing the banjo. Pretty cool, huh?"*

Practicing

From the time when we were young and practicing clarinet or piano for an hour a day, many of us had the feeling that we'd rather be outside playing than inside tackling Czerny exercises to get our gold star at the end of the week. On the other hand, people generally take up the banjo because they're drawn to it for recreational or therapeutic reasons, or both.

People sometimes ask me how much time they should allot for daily practice. I tell them that there is no exact answer; if pressed, I recommend an hour a day if job, school and family commitments allow. Before I had kids, I would set aside a certain block of time to practice. If I wasn't enjoying myself, I would just plow through my practice routine in order to stick to my self-imposed schedule. Béla Fleck once told me that he'd pick up the banjo whenever the mood struck him and put it down when he felt like he'd had enough. Either plan can work; it depends on what best suits you.

One simple but effective practice incentive is to simply leave your banjo out in full view. You'll be more apt to gravitate toward your instrument when it's right there in your face. Duke Ellington used to talk about walking past the piano at midnight on his way to bed and experiencing a "seduction." He would then sit down and spend the next four hours creating a new piece of music. To allow yourself a continuing series of seductions, I recommend keeping your instrument in its *open* case in a room that you frequent.

You can also keep your banjo on a guitar stand. Purchase a "gravity" stand or some other very stable stand that allows the banjo to hang by the headstock and rest against the rubber-coated legs. The other common style of stand has a moveable "wishbone" arrangement on which the bottom of the banjo rests. I had one of these once, and it was so unstable that my banjo fell off, snapping the headstock. Some wishbone stands come with a rubber strap to hold the neck. When using one of these, take extra care to ensure that your instrument is securely in place.

Where to Begin
When practicing, I always begin with metronome work so that I can feel totally locked in rhythmically, no matter what I'm playing. I warm up by spending five or ten minutes using the metronome as I work on exercises with both the left and right hands.

Playing Through Tunes
After this warm-up, what you practice is up to you. You might spend half an hour on new material, then another 15 minutes using the metronome as you brush up on old tunes or techniques. After you've been playing for a while, you may find that you forget certain tunes. Don't worry about this; if you've started to play with other people, you'll find that certain tunes work their way into your repertoire, and you'll probably remember those. If you just play by yourself, you'll have certain favorites that you gravitate toward, while others fall away.

BANJO MASTERS SPEAK: Alan Munde

"As a lifetime student of music and as a teacher of the banjo, I have encountered many frustrating moments. One mission I'm on is to assure new arrivals to the banjo that, as daunting as it may seem for a beginner, it is doable. A student has to be able to follow very specific, detailed instructions, put in a large amount of time to train the muscles to move in exact ways and train the brain to recognize melodies, rhythms, harmonies and limitless subtleties in the music. I have witnessed many students of all ages who have become much better players than they ever thought possible. How long will it take? It takes as long as it takes, and a student should develop an attitude that the lifetime investment of time, concentration and energy is worth the incredibly pleasurable payoff of personal music making."

Keep an alphabetically organized binder of all of the tablature-notated pieces you have so that you can easily access tunes that may have drifted from your memory. For tunes that you've learned by ear rather than by TAB, you might want to make recordings and keep them in the same place as your TAB notebook.

When you practice a tune, take note of both the section that you have the most difficulty with and the speed at which you're playing it. Rather than going through something at a moderate to fast speed and slowing down for a tricky section, play everything at a tempo you can maintain throughout. Of course, just for fun, you can try to play things quickly once in a while; however, playing a tune at a consistent tempo will help you develop a solid rhythmic foundation. Pay attention to every note that you play; good playing is all in the details. Make sure every note is absolutely clean, that you're happy with the tone and that you're in time. Don't let yourself make a mistake and go on. Be as self-aware as you can be.

Looping
Looping is a useful practice technique. When you have a problem with a particular series of notes or a particular measure, don't play the entire tune over and over, hoping to make it through the difficult section. Instead, "loop" the problem area—repeat that measure or section five or ten times with the metronome set at a slow tempo until you can play it correctly and cleanly. Try the whole piece again at a speed that's comfortable. More often than not, the problem will have dissolved; if not, repeat the process.

Playing with Recordings
Try using part of your practice time to play along with recordings. Playing along with a recording has a number of benefits. It forces you to keep up, but if you get off track along the way, you can still find your way back, and all in real time. It will also allow you to get a good sense of the melody that you may retain when you solo. On a recording, you will hear cues from other instruments, for example, guitar or bass runs that lead you into the next chord. Perhaps most importantly, you'll learn to play while in the midst (at least sonically) of other musicians. This may initially be a distracting experience, but with practice it will become second nature and will teach you to listen as you play.

Exploring
Spend part of your practice time noodling around, exploring the fingerboard, discovering new positions on your own, trying to write a tune or improvising. Loosen up and see what flows out. During workshops I sometimes have students place their fingers on the neck in a "random" position they've never used before. You don't even have to listen as you're getting your fingers set. Once you've established a position, use a simple roll to activate the strings, and see (and hear) what comes out. You may find that you've created something completely discordant or, instead, something incredibly beautiful. In either case, make sure to incorporate the 5th string to see how it sounds in relationship with the other notes. Try letting go of one of your left-hand fingers to see how the chord sounds with an open string. You can also move a finger up or down a fret, or fret the 5th string with your thumb. Take chances, and see what happens.

Chapter 6

Left-Hand Techniques

So far we've focused mainly on important right-hand techniques. Now, let's take a closer look at the left hand. Not only is the left hand responsible for chord fingerings, but you can also spiff up your solos with left-hand techniques like slides, pull-offs and hammer-ons. In addition to adding color to your playing, each of these techniques can play an important role in rhythm and timing.

The Slide

The *slide* is a left-hand technique that lends a somewhat vocal quality and a sense of heightened emotion to your playing. In practical terms, it's the movement of one of your left-hand fingers from one fret to another after a string has been plucked. By plucking a string once and executing a slide, you'll get one or two extra notes for your effort. (For a good demonstration of slides, listen to *Boil Them Cabbage Down*, Track 42 on the accompanying CD. You'll hear seven of them in the space of one pass through the tune.)

The most common slide involves moving from the 2nd fret to the 3rd fret on the 3rd string.

39
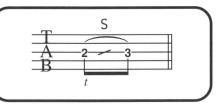

S = Slide

In the next example, you'll start with simple quarter notes and progress to a slide incorporated into a square roll. There are two ways to perform the slide as part of a roll. I prefer to slide as I simultaneously hit the 2nd string. Some players like a quick slide, which anticipates the playing of the 2nd string. In either case, make sure your right hand holds down the rhythmic fort. Don't slow down to wait for the left hand. Also, be sure to lift your finger away from the fingerboard immediately after each slide; this will give you a cleaner, less clashing sound.

40

Track 41

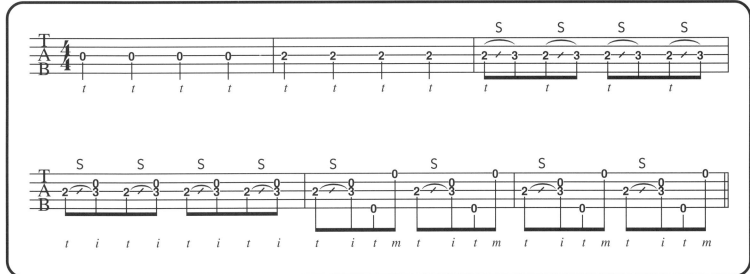

Boil Them Cabbage Down is a perfect tune for demonstrating the slide's potential for adding a more vocal and, in this case, bluesy quality to a melody. In addition to introducing the slide, we'll also use a new chord, D, as a substitute for the D7. Fret it like this:

41

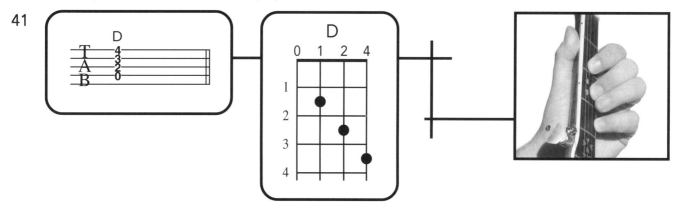

Start boiling:

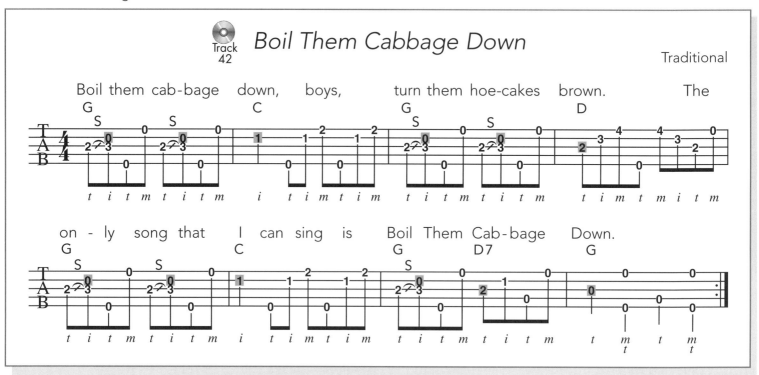

Old Dan Tucker (see page 37) is another chestnut that employs the slide. Here you can really see and hear the modular aspect of the bluegrass style, wherein certain licks make their way from one tune to another. The lick in this case is the square-roll slide, the same one that recurs throughout *Boil Them Cabbage Down*. In this version of *Old Dan Tucker*, we'll also use the slide in a forward roll combined with a quarter-note pinch to bring out the melody.

Old Dan Tucker

Track 43

Traditional

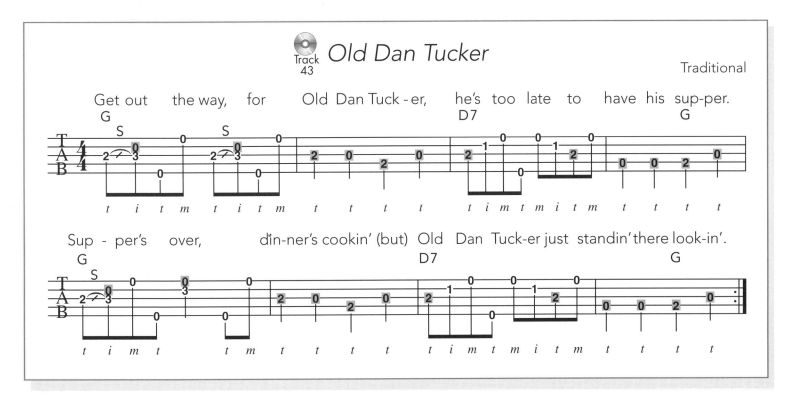

You can also integrate the slide into a forward-backward roll.

42 Track 44

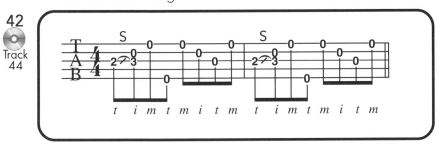

Georgia Buck is a wonderful old-time tune that appears in a number of different musical traditions. Here we'll use both square rolls and forward-backward rolls to bring out the slide.

Georgia Buck

Track 45

Traditional

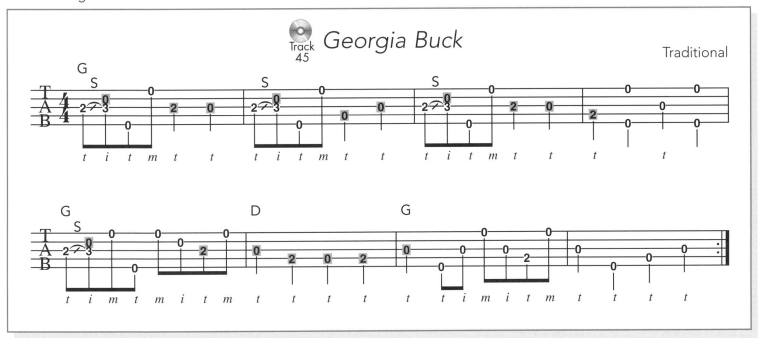

The Hammer-On

As its name implies, the *hammer-on* involves picking a string and then forcefully bringing down a left-hand finger on the string, effectively fretting it after it has already been plucked.

43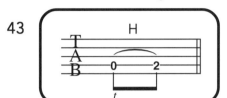

H = Hammer-on

You can use the hammer-on on either an open string or a string that another finger has already fretted further down the neck. In the next example, you'll use the open-string hammer-on. I like to hammer on the 4th and 3rd strings with my 2nd finger, the 2nd string with my 1st finger and the 1st string with my 3rd finger. Take care to make all eighth notes equal.

44
Track 46
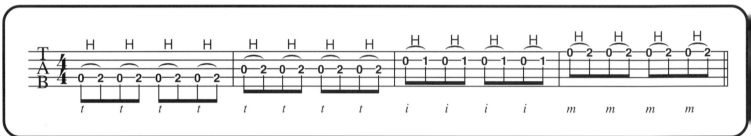

I now respectfully present the immortal *Hammer-On Teapot Etude:*

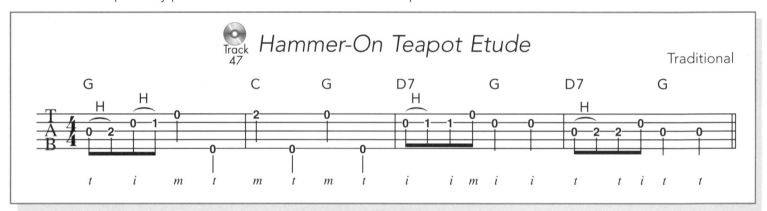

Ideally, the note you're hammering on should be as loud as the note that you pick. You may not be able to achieve this at first, but it's a goal to work toward. Well-executed and clear hammered-on notes are another of the important details that are key in achieving a professional sound.

Like some of the moves you've already learned, hammer-ons can spiff up a roll pattern, as in the exercise below. Heed the same advice I gave you when you incorporated the slide into rolls: Don't drag, and be vigilant in keeping the rolls even. Pick the 2nd string simultaneously with the 2nd note in the hammer-on. Use your 2nd finger to hammer, and keep it down throughout the square roll.

45
Track 48
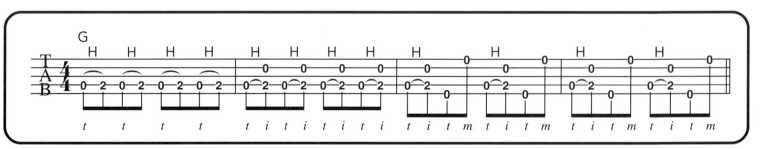

The hammer-on also works with forward rolls.

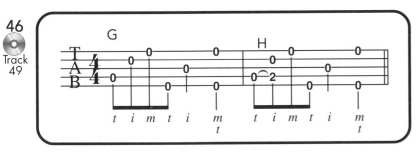

Cumberland Gap is a fine old fiddle tune that features some 4th-string hammer-ons.
Don't forget to observe the repeat signs.

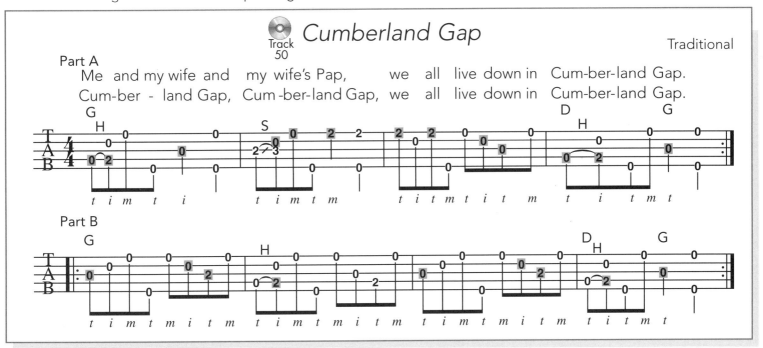

If you were restricted by some cruel, malevolent force to playing only one banjo tune for
the rest of your life, the tune would probably have to be *Cripple Creek*, which is in the
repertoire of every self-respecting banjo player. In this version, you'll find more slides,
plus the hammer-on lick you just used in *Cumberland Gap*. Once again, you can see that
even a somewhat limited repertoire of licks is useful in many different situations.

The Pull-Off

The *pull-off* is the last (but certainly not the least) of the "big three" left-hand maneuvers. To execute a pull-off, fret a string with a left-hand finger, pick the string with the right hand and either pull down (away from you, in toward your palm) or push up (toward you, away from your palm) with the left-hand finger. The note you'll end up on will be either an open string or a lower-pitched fretted string (for example, when you pull off from the 3rd fret to the 2nd fret of the 3rd string).

Ideally, as in the hammer-on, the note you pull off to will be as loud as the one you initially picked. Don't just lift your finger straight off the fingerboard; instead, give the string a little snap as you move your finger away. Pull-offs can be a little more difficult to master than hammer-ons; you can get some excellent practice by trying some pull-offs on the 1st string.

P = Pull-off

When playing Exercise 48, use the 2nd or 3rd finger of your left hand. Pull off the edge of the banjo neck to get a nice snap. Make sure that you play the pull-offs as even eighth notes.

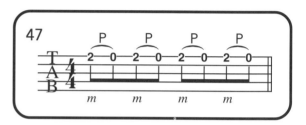

Now try the pull-off on each of the first four strings. Use your 3rd finger on the 1st string, your 1st finger on the 2nd string and your 2nd finger on the 3rd and 4th strings. For now, don't worry about hitting adjoining strings as you pull off. It's an occupational hazard, but it also indicates that you're moving your fingers in the right direction, rather than lifting them straight off the fingerboard. As in the preceding example, I recommend that you pull down off the 1st string, because there's no adjoining string to get in your way. For the other pull-offs you can either push up or pull down. (For this exercise, I pull down on all of them, but try it both ways.) Make sure you get under each string enough to get the characteristic snap.

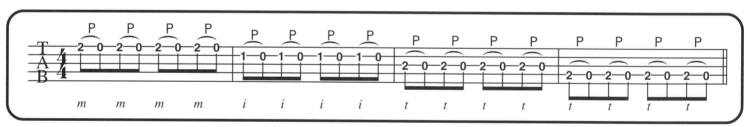

Here's an old-time-style tune I made up to illustrate the pull-off in a musical context.

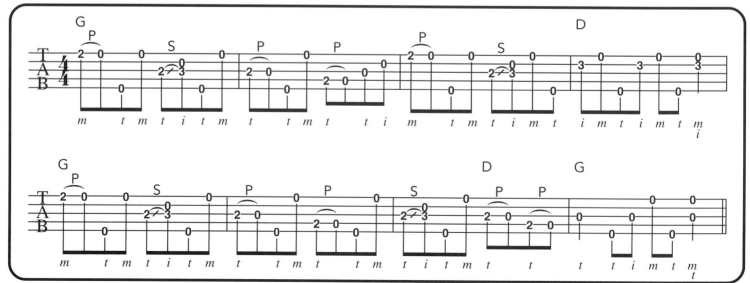

Half Steps and Whole Steps

In thinking about scales and keys, it's helpful to understand that we can measure the distance between notes. The closest distance between any two notes is a *half step*, which on the banjo is a distance of one fret. For example, the distance from the 1st fret to the 2nd fret is one half step. The distance of two half steps—two frets—is called a *whole step*. For example, the distance from the 1st fret to the 3rd is a whole step.

Scales

A *scale* is a series of notes arranged in a specific order of whole steps and half steps. A note takes its name from the letter of its pitch, that is, A, B, C, D, E, F or G. The notes of a scale ascend in alphabetical order; following G, the names begin again at A. The specific position of each note within a scale is called the *scale degree*. Scale degrees are numbered beginning with 1 on the lowest note, and progress upward from there.

Major Scales

A *major scale* is made up of eight notes with half steps between the 3rd and 4th, and 7th and 8th degrees. The rest are whole steps. A scale takes its name from its lowest note (or 1st degree); for example, the C Major scale is named for its first note, C. The eight notes of the scale span an *octave*, which is the closest distance between any two notes with the same name (12 half steps); in other words, the 8th degree is an octave above the 1st degree. Study the placement of whole and half steps represented by the letters "W" and "H" in the following diagram of the C Major scale. The first C (Middle C) is not playable on the banjo in standard bluegrass tuning. It is included here to show the pattern of half steps and whole steps that make up the C Major scale.

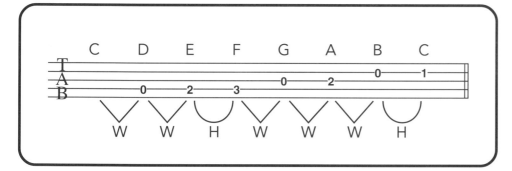

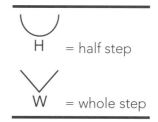

Keys

When all the chords and notes in a tune are from the same scale, such as the C Major scale, they are said to be in the same *key*, for example, C Major. So far, everything we've played has been in the key of G. While the key of G is the virtual playground for bluegrass banjo, the five-string can also have a field day in other keys. On the banjo, the unique sound of a particular key is closely tied to the relationship between fretted and open strings. The note G of the open third string has a different meaning in the key of G, in which it is the first note of the scale, than in it does in the key of C, in which G is the fifth note of the scale.

The I-IV-V

When you speak of the key of G, it means that the G Major chord is the focal point, the center of gravity. It's as if G Major were the sun and all other chords in relation to it—so far, mainly C and D (or D7)—were orbiting planets. As we begin to talk about the key of C, the C Major chord takes the lead, while the F and G (or G7) chords play supporting roles.

This raises the topic of the I–IV–V, a chord progression that is a staple of musical styles and periods from Baroque to bluegrass. To review, the three primary chords in the key of G are G, C and D. G is called the I chord because it's built on the first note of the scale. The C chord, built on the fourth note of the scale, is called the IV chord. You've probably guessed that the D, built on the fifth note of the scale, is the V chord.

Though the actual chords will change from one key to the next, the relative relationships among and functions of the I, IV and V remain the same. In the key of C, for example, the I, IV and V are used in the same way as they are in G. Using the same principle as above, however, the actual chords are C (I), F (IV) and G (V).

Let's begin to explore the key of C by carting out a chord progression you already know from a tune you already know (*Boil Them Cabbage Down*); now, though, you'll strum it in the new key.

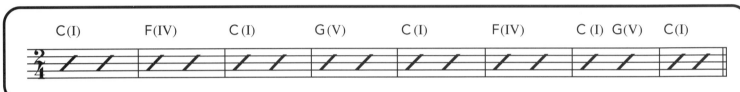

Here's another tune to give you the feel of the key of C. I found a tune called *Tiddley Winks Dance* in a 1923 book by Septimus Winner, *The Eureka Method for the Banjo*. *Tiddley Winks Dance* became the inspiration for the A section of this next ditty, which I've titled *New Tiddley Winks Dance*.

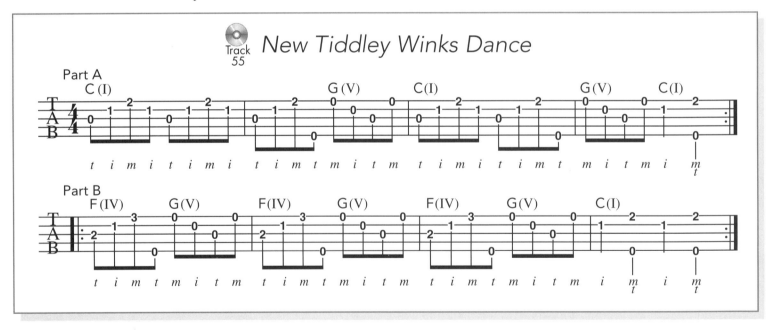

There is a story of a banjo player who, when asked if he could read music, replied, "not enough to hurt my playing." While it's true that many of the most revered bluegrass banjoists don't read standard music notation, the ability to read music will expand your musical horizons immeasurably. There are grain silos full of banjo music written in the 19th and 20th centuries that exists only in standard notation. So that you might have a chance to explore the pleasures that all of this music offers, here's a crash course in reading music.

Standard notation isn't much more difficult to learn than TAB is. In my years of teaching, I've found that a good number of people have, at one time or another, taken lessons on piano, clarinet or other instruments and learned to read music in the process. They may need to jog their memories to remember the ins and outs of standard notation, but in just about every case, the ability to read music comes back to them when they apply their musical knowledge to the banjo. If you never learned music notation on another instrument, it'll take just a minute to learn the basics and apply them to the five-string.

Anatomy of the Staff

Standard notation makes use of a five-line staff. (It is important to note that the horizontal lines in this staff have a completely different meaning from those in TAB.) Banjoists always read from a staff with a *treble clef*, which is shown at right.

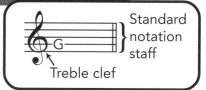

Notice that the bottom part of the treble clef loops around second-lowest line of the staff. This line represents the note G (the treble clef is also called the *G clef*), and all other notes on the staff are named relative to this fixed point. Each line and space represents a different note; for example, the space above the G is the note A, the line above that the note B, etc. (See pages 5 and 41 for a review of the musical alphabet.) Notes are indicated with oval *note heads*. The treble clef indicates this particular arrangement of notes on the lines of the staff:

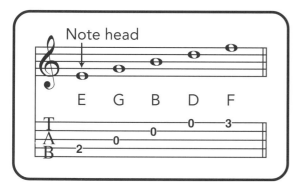

The time-honored phrase that will help you remember this bottom-to-top arrangement of E–G–B–D–F is "**E**very **G**ood **B**oy **D**eserves **F**udge." (Perhaps "**E**arl's **G**reat **B**anjo **D**eserves **F**avor" is more appropriate for our purposes.) Use one of these as a memory aid, or make up one of your own.

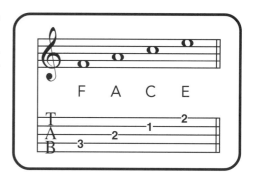

The spaces between the lines also indicate specific notes. As you can see at right, the notes in the spaces of the staff spell out the word "face."

The last two notes you'll need to know for now are the notes in the spaces just below and above the staff—D and G, respectively.

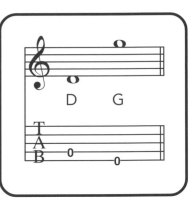

If you were to visualize all of these notes together, in ascending order, here's how they'd look, both on a keyboard and on a treble staff. (The note Middle C isn't found on the banjo in standard bluegrass tuning; it's included here as a point of reference.)

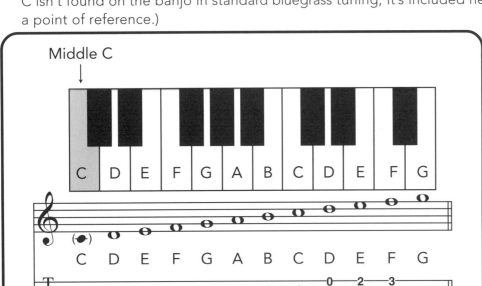

Relating TAB and Standard Notation

Let's look at the notes of the banjo's open strings in G tuning, starting with the lowest-sounding string, to see how TAB relates to standard notation. As a matter of convenience in conventional notation, banjo notes on the treble staff sound an *octave* lower (at the same pitch but in a lower range) than they are written.

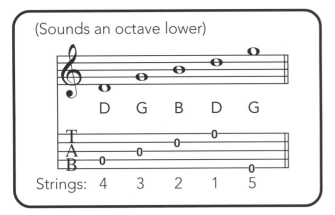

Eighth and quarter notes in standard notation are similar in appearance to those in TAB, except that oval note heads take the place of numbers in the staff.

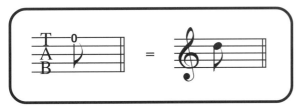

Now let's play a modified forward-backward roll written in both standard notation and TAB. Try to read the notated staff without referring to the TAB; take it slow and be conscious of each note you play.

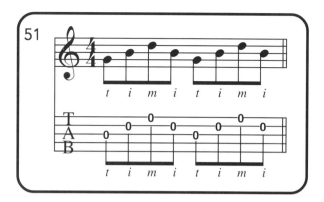

The next tune dates from the early days of the banjo. The *Easy Jig* on page 46, which is from S. S. Stewart's *The Minstrel Banjoist* (1881), uses a notational shortcut you'll sometimes encounter in older banjo music. You'll see that some notes have flags, even though they are already beamed as eighth notes. These are not "rhythmic" flags; they merely indicate that the note is the open-fifth-string G.

Here's a diagram of the notes you'll need, with their TAB equivalents:

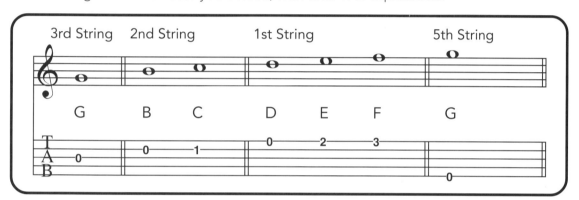

*A member of the Virginia group Cloud Valley in the 1980s, **Bill Evans** has also toured and recorded with Dry Branch Fire Squad. Evans, a Rounder recording artist and an incredibly versatile banjoist and musicologist, has played in styles ranging from minstrel to progressive.*

BANJO MASTERS SPEAK: Bill Evans

"Your first banjo doesn't have to be an expensive instrument by any means, but it is good to have one that's set up well. In order for you to develop the proper right-hand technique, it's important to have a banjo bridge that's at least 5/8" tall. Some beginners' banjos have bridges that are significantly lower, and this can cramp your right hand. The string action—or the height of the strings from the fingerboard—is something that varies from one banjo to the next. There's no need to worry about this too much, unless it's way too low or too high.

"In general, it helps to seek out a music store in your area that's knowledgeable about bluegrass and banjos in order to get assistance with setting up your instrument. Even if you have to drive a bit to get to a good store, it's usually worth the effort. The store may also be able to connect you with a good teacher as well as provide a point of entrée into the regional bluegrass jam and festival scene."

And now, the *Easy Jig.*

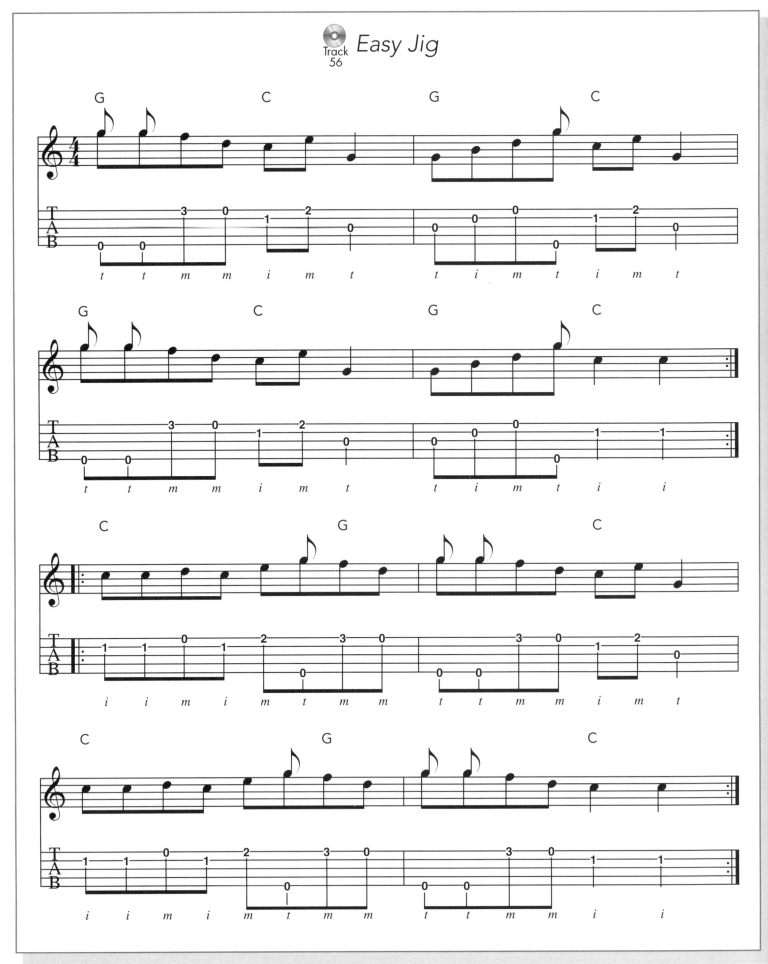

Appendix

Need a Banjo?

If you've bought this book, chances are you already own or have borrowed a banjo. If not, here are a couple of suggestions. Unless you have plenty of expendable cash, you probably aren't looking to drop two to three thousand dollars on a top-of the-line instrument. In the old days, low-end banjos were often available new in pawn shops for anywhere between one hundred and three hundred dollars. The problem was that you never knew whether you were getting a lemon or a diamond in the rough. I once had a student who bought a hundred-dollar plastic banjo that blew away most thousand-dollar instruments. You never know.

As of this writing, however, the guesswork in buying a banjo is gone. Thanks to excellent makers like Deering and Goldtone, you can be assured of getting a good-sounding, quality instrument for between three hundred and four hundred dollars. Both firms sell open-back and resonated instruments. For bluegrass, I usually recommend resonator-style banjos (which come with a slightly higher price tag), because their louder tone is better suited to playing in an ensemble context.

Other Resources

Recordings
As I've said, listening is one of the most important things you can do. Since space limitations prevent the inclusion of a full-blown discography, I've instead included contact information for two great mail order companies that offer a wide range of banjo recordings:

County Sales
Main Street
Floyd, VA 24091
540-745-2001
www.countysales.com

Copper Creek
P.O. Box 3161
Roanoake, VA 24015
1-888-438-2448
www.coppercreekrec.com

Publications
The following publications are indispensable for banjo enthusiasts:

Banjo Newsletter
P.O. Box 3148
Annapolis, MD 21403-0418
1-800-759-7425
www.banjonews.com

Bluegrass Unlimited
P.O. Box 771
Warrenton, VA 20188-0771
1-800-BLU-GRAS
www.bluegrassmusic.com

BANJO MASTERS SPEAK: J. D. Crowe

"Learn to tune. That's essential, accurate tuning. Then you have the three Ts: tone, timing, taste. Find the placement of your hand on the head where you think the instrument sounds best. Play the melody of the song. Pay attention to the separation of notes in a roll. Make every note clean, not muffled, and solid as you can; this relates to playing the melody more than anything. Don't try to put too much into it when you first start out. Learn the basics before you learn the real flashy stuff. Starting off with [that kind of playing] is hard to do as a beginner. Of course, it all depends on the individual, what his ears like, because everyone's different."